How To Attract Success

By

F. W. SEARS, M.P.

AUTHOR OF

"THE BOOKS WITHOUT AN IF SERIES,"
"How to Give Treatments," "New Thought Lectures," Vols. I and II,
"How We Create Ourselves," "The Law of Cause and Effect,"
"The Unpardonable Sin," "Reincarnation—Why, When,
Where?" "Death!—Then What?" "The Law of
Abundance," "The Resurrection of the
Body," "The Risen Self," "The Secret
of Healing," "What Creates En-
vironment," "Our Judgment
Days," "What is God,"
etc., etc.

CENTRE PUBLISHING CO.
NEW YORK

———

L. N. FOWLER & CO.
LONDON, ENG.

———

TABLE OF CONTENTS

CHAPTER IV.

CHAPTER V.

CHAPTER VI.

PUBLISHERS' STATEMENT

To the Purchaser:

It is a self-evident fact that you wanted to get something out of this book or you would not have purchased it.

Therefore the first thing to do before you begin to read is to relax and become receptive to the lessons it teaches.

The second thing is to read slowly and try to *absorb* its lessons rather than learn them mentally.

The third thing is to remember that this book only *teaches* how to grow a constructive and harmonious consciousness; *you* will have to do the work of *applying* its lessons.

New habits are not formed in a day and the lessons which this book teaches will not be absorbed in one reading. The student who will devote not less than half an hour each day to their study and then *apply* them in living his daily life will receive untold benefit. It is dependent on *you alone* as to how valuable this book becomes to you.

The author has proven for himself everything he teaches. *He knows that everything he says is true,* and *you can know it* too but *you* will have to *apply* the lessons and prove them for yourself.

You will note that the author does not quote any "authorities" for any of his statements. The highest authority any soul can possibly have is its own God-self and it is this God-self in you which the proper and persistent study and application of these lessons will bring out into greater expression, and thus enable you to set the new causes in motion which will bring you success along any line you may desire.

THE PUBLISHERS.

AUTHOR'S STATEMENT.

Many books and treatises have been written on the subject of " Success " and the methods to be used in obtaining it. These works have been the honest statements of their authors who have used and found them successful. The student, in attempting to apply them, has usually been successful for a while but the day invariably came when he found that something was lacking, and the same methods which formerly brought success failed him in his need.

In the business world it has always been considered that the salesman who could sell a customer "something he did not want" was the best salesman. Men are taught "Business Psychology," which consists in controlling the "other fellow's " mind through the power of " Mental suggestion " and *making* him do what the salesman wants.

The world has not realized that the Law of Force was the controlling factor in these methods and that we can only retain a thing under the same Law by which it is obtained.

To be successful in anything one must be able to *retain* as well as *obtain* it; he must also be able to *obtain* it when he wants it, where he wants it, and be able to *retain* it as long as he wants it.

It is obvious then that when we *obtain* anything under the Law of Force we must be prepared to exert our Force all the time to a geater degree than can anyone else in order to be able to *obtain* what we want, when and where we want it, and to *retain* it as long as we want it.

Few men, that is few in comparison with the entire population of the world, are able to maintain this Law of Force against all comers for any great length of time, and so we have failure after failure. Some are able to maintain it for only a few months, others for several years, while those who are able to maintain it for a life-time against all-comers usually do so through making a sort of "truce" or combination—Trust—with others of their kind.

In this book is taught the true Law of Success, which is the "Law of Harmonious Attraction." Under this Law things come to us "because they *want* to come" and not because "we *make* them come;" they remain with us because they "*want* to do so." Instead of working to control the "other fellow" we learn to control ourselves and become so strong, powerful and harmonious in our attractive power that the things we want will "*want* us" so much that they cannot remain away.

The salesman who uses this Law finds that he is led to those who *want* to buy his goods, instead of to those whom he has to *force* into buying. The result is that he has a satisfied clientele instead of a dissatisfied one; that instead of having to dodge around the corner when he sees a former customer approaching, he goes up to meet him knowing that he will receive a hearty welcome and probably be given information which will help him make other sales.

The business man who uses this Law can go to bed at night with his mind free from the fear that he may wake up in the morning and find himself a pauper because his investments have proven to be bad or that some confidential clerk has absconded with his wealth.

The person who uses this Law to obtain Happiness or any other ideal will find that he has not been chasing an "ignus fatus" which disappears just as he thinks he has obtained it.

It is impossible for one working under any other Law to take away from us what we have gained under the Law of Harmonious Attraction, for this is the strongest and most powerful Law in the Universe; while those working under this Law will never *want* to take it away from us.

The Law of Harmonious Attraction, and the other Laws referred to in this book, are not new Laws, and the Author claims nothing for their discovery; they have existed throughout all time and have been used unconsciously to a greater or less extent throughout all the ages. The only claim the Author makes is for their revival and their conscious application by mankind along all lines, and the new application of them which he teaches.

The Author would teach the same common sense application of these Laws to the *energy which creates things* that the world uses in the handling of these things after they are created. Thus when one leaves his home he locks the doors and fastens the windows in order to prevent intruders from gaining entrance and stealing his valuables, but in his thought world he leaves the doors and windows open to all the thieves, tramps and vagabonds of the destructive thought currents. Man should learn to lock the " doors and windows " of his thought world against the "thieves and vagabonds"—vicious thoughts of all kinds—of that plane by forming the *fixed habit* of displacing them by constructive and harmonious thinking.

To the thousands of hungry souls that have battled long enough with the world under the Law of Force and who are ready to learn the larger Truth of the Law of Harmonious Attraction, is this book dedicated. All such will read and re-read it hundreds of times, get into the vibrations from which it was written and receive their own message of Harmony direct from the one great Source. Those who have not been beaten to earth again and again by the reaction of the Law of Force on their own lives and who are not ready for the great Truths contained herein will go on under their old Law, setting more and more destructive causes in motion until they too cry out for mercy and say, "Oh, God! Why hast thou forsaken me." Sometime they too will learn the lesson that "no one can save us from our own Laws but ourselves."

THE AUTHOR.

HOW TO ATTRACT SUCCESS.

F. W. SEARS, M. P.
GENERAL LECTURER,
THE NEW THOUGHT CHURCH, INC.
NEW YORK.

CHAPTER I.

WHAT IS SUCCESS?—THE LAWS THAT MAKE FOR
SUCCESS.—"DECLARING WAR ON POVERTY."—
MUST "BUILD CASTLES IN THE AIR" BEFORE
CASTLES CAN BE BUILT ON THE GROUND.—EF-
FECT OF ENVIRONMENT.—FIXED HABITS.—
WHAT "GOOD LUCK" AND "BAD LUCK" IS.—
MAN IS AN UNCONSCIOUS CREATOR BUT CAN
BECOME A CONSCIOUS ONE.—WHAT MAKES
THE DIFFERENCE BETWEEN PERSONS.—HOW
TO CREATE AND ATTRACT SUCCESS PER-
MANENTLY.

What is success? To be successful in
anything is to have the ability and power

to do the thing we want to do when and where we want to do it, or to have what we want, when we want it and as long as we want it.

Success is a thing which we can build for just as surely and as scientifically as the architect plans and builds the skyscraper or the engineer the wonderful tunnels and bridges of modern times.

The Laws which make for success are just as natural—although less generally understood—as are the laws which the architect and engineer use in their work.

A New York paper, in a recent editorial on "Declaring War on Poverty," among other things said, "Why then, does not the war begin? There is no reason—save the lack of organization for such a crusade. The men who want to abolish poverty, who know that it can be abolished

and are able to abolish it, have not yet
found a common standard around which
to recruit their forces."

No, and they never will find a " common
standard " until they learn the great
truth that *everything begins and ends in con-*
sciousness—in the thought world, the imagination, for that is where man does all
his imaging—and that until the individual gets rid of a poverty consciousness, a
poverty image, he will never be free permanently from a poverty environment.

Within each life lies the causes of whatever enters into it. Man is building his
own world every moment of his life. He
creates from with-in the energy which attracts from with-out. The thoughts he
thinks are his own private property and
they generate the power with which he
builds from with-in and attracts from with-

out. Like builds like and like attracts like. Man must first have "castles in the air" before he can have castles on the ground.

It is true that the man who is kept busy at good wages and given a pleasant and comfortable environment has the *external* things and conditions which will help him create a consciousness or image of abundance, but until he has *established* the *fixed habit* of *thinking constructively*, he will not continue to stay out of a poverty-stricken environment indefinitely.

Was the giving of a pleasant and comfortable environment to man and providing him with continuous employment an insurance against poverty the solution would be simple, easy and sure of quick accomplishment.

But we know that such a remedy has

never effected a permanent cure; that *something more* than employment and environment is necessary. We know many men who have started out in life with everything their hearts could wish in both of these things, but the day came when their employment was gone and their environment poverty stricken.

What was it they lacked? What is that "something more" which is so necessary to the peace, happiness and success of man?

We have called it "bad luck," or rather the want of "good luck" heretofore, but it is neither. In the past we have been of the belief that success along any line was largely a matter of chance, or luck, but we know better to-day. We *know* that there is no such thing as either chance or luck, good or bad, in the universe.

" Good luck " is simply the effect of constructive and harmonious causes we have unconsciously set in motion sometime previous to its occurrence, while " bad luck " is the effect of destructive and inharmonious causes we have just as unconsciously set in motion and which we have not yet learned how to antidote or displace.

To-day we know that success is the consciousness of the abundance of supply and the recognition of our *oneness* with it. We may *believe* in the truth of this but until we *know* it beyond any question of a doubt it is impossible to materialize the belief at all times and under all circumstances.

We *know* that the things we have called luck, accident, chance, etc., simply *seem* so on the surface—on the external side of life—because we have only looked for their causes on the objective side; but when we look back of the external and go deeply into the energy which produced them we learn that all these so-called accidents, chance, luck, are the natural effects of natural Laws; that these Laws are as simple and easily understood as is the law that one and one makes two.

Before a spade is stuck into the ground in excavating for one of our immense skyscrapers the building has been entirely finished, even to the last coat of paint on the walls, in the consciousness—the thought world, the imagination—of the architect.

Before even one screw, nut, or bolt was made for the engines which generate the power on our ocean greyhounds the entire engine was completed in the consciousness—the thought world, the imagination —of the engineer who drafted the plans.

Both architect and engineer built " castles in the air" first, before their " air castles " could be materialized in objective form.

The engine which generates the steam does not know for what purpose the energy is to be used, and the masses have no greater knowledge of the use to which they will put the energy they create than does the engine; they work as unconsciously and as ignorantly of the effects of the energy they generate as does the engine.

Man, however, can become a conscious creator while the engine cannot, and in the consciousness or knowledge of this power does man have the advantage. When he neglects to develop or does not use his power, the effect is as disastrous to him as to the engine, for when the engine

lies idle any length of time it rusts, be·
comes useless and fit only for the scrap
pile. So with man, for when he fails to use
his faculties and power they become atro·
phied from disuse and he too soon rusts
out and becomes only fit for the scrap pile.
On the other hand when man does de·
velop and use his power the effect becomes
more beneficial to him than to the engine.

Man is an individual creator; he not
only creates his body but he also creates
his environment.

MAN POSSESSES WITHIN HIMSELF ALL THE
CREATIVE POWER OF THE UNIVERSE. This is
a most stupendous statement, one which
the masses cannot understand nor comprehend fully in their present state of consciousness, but each life may develop itself to where it not only understands but
knows this truth. The only difference be·

tween persons is in the amount of this creative power each life expresses harmoniously.

There is absolutely nothing we have ever had in the past, have now, or ever will have, but what we have created for ourselves. Most of us have done the larger part of our work of creating unconsciously and ignorantly, and we have not stopped to see, study, and understand the relationship between the use we made of this energy and the things it has created for us. It has been so much easier to blame the disastrous effects to chance, accident, or luck.

On the objective plane we have learned that a sharp knife, drawn across the hand, cuts it; but what we have not yet learned is that when we *think* vicious thoughts of any kind—fear, worry, anger, hatred, re-

sentment, resistance, impatience, intolerance, condemnation, criticism, envy, jealousy, etc.—such thoughts generate an energy which causes us to relate with the
things on the objective plane, both in the
physical body and its environment, that we
do not want. It is this relationship of
effect to cause which we must learn before
we can begin to permanently abolish
poverty or anything else we do not want.

Now do not understand that it is impossible to abolish poverty *temporarily,* or
even for a lifetime in *some* lives, without
either a knowledge or application of this
truth, for such is not the case.

Some few lives—few as compared with
the multitude of persons living at any
time—may concentrate their entire creative power on the subject of money and
amass great wealth and hold it too during

their life in any incarnation and still
think all these vicious thoughts and manifest them objectively, but "Be not de-
ceived, for God—the great Universal Law
—is not mocked, and whatsoever a man
soweth that also shall he reap," and in the
incarnations yet to come for such a life
will it reap the effects of the energy it has
created, either in poverty, sickness, or
misery of some kind.

The object of these lessons is to teach
how to create and attract success to us
permanently—not temporarily; how to
get what we want, get it when we want it,
and keep it as long as we want it. When
we know this Law, and it becomes such a
fixed habit in our lives that we live it as
unconsciously as we are now living, live it
because we have developed such a consciousness that we do not know how to

live any other way, there will be no need
for "declaring war on poverty," disease,
or misery, for we will then cease to gen-
eate the energy which relates us with
these things.

Every moment of our lives, with every
breath we draw, we are creating something.] There has never been a second of
time, all along down the ages past and
gone, in which we have not created something for ourselves.

We are to-day, in body and environment, the effects of these creations of our
past. We want to *know* this *now*. We also
want to *know* that we will continue to
create ourselves and our environment all
down the future ages yet to come, not
only here in this world but also in all the
worlds through which we have yet to
evolve in our return to our Source.

With this understanding thoroughly fixed in our consciousness let us learn how we may create consciously for success, and attract it to us under such Laws as will make it permanent in our lives.

CHAPTER II.

How Man May be Classified.—Different Degrees of Unfoldment.—The Five General States of Consciousness.—What the "Sub-conscious Mind" Really Is.—The Mind of the Physical Body.—The Mind of the Ego or Astral Body.—The True Function of "Logic."—Mind of Physical Body Makes the Conditions by Which Mind of Astral Body May Manifest In and Through the Physical Body.—What the Imagination Is and its Proper Function.—"Impressions" and "Intuitions": Their Source, and How to Tell "Which is Which."

Man may be classified in a general way as being composed of five entirely different states of consciousness, degrees of unfoldment, or conditions of development, viz: Instinct, Intellect, Inspiration, Intuition, and Revelation. Bear in mind, how-

ever, that while the Instinct is a manifestation of the Physical plane, the Intellect of the Mental, the Inspirational
of the Soul, the Intuitional and Revelational of the Spiritual, all these states
of conciousness are just as much spiritual
as is the latter, the difference being that
they do not *express* as much. It is like
ice, water, clouds and the invisible vapor,
they are all one and the same but differ
in their expression.

Most persons are over-developed in one
of these states of consciousness and under-developed in the others, and that is
why it is so hard for them to understand
the other states. Few persons are so
equally developed in all of them as to be
able to impart their knowledge of the Inspirational, Intuitional and Revelational
planes in such a way as may be under-

stood by those manifesting only on the planes of Instinct and Intellect.

On the Physical plane of consciousness man expresses what is called "instinct." This is the "cell consciousness" referred to more at length in my lectures on "How We Create Ourselves," "How to Give Treatments," and others. This "cell consciousness"—which is really the intelligence in the cells of the physical body and in the atoms of the environment—is the only consciousness which is under the direction and control of the intellect and is therefore in reality the only "sub-conscious mind" there is, for the ego's mind is never subject to the conscious mind or intellect.

In the creating, destroying, re-creating and re-destroying of our bodies—which process is going on continuously every moment of our lives, awake or asleep—we attract to us atoms which will express the same degree of intelligence as those which harmonize with the energy we are momentarily creating by the thoughts we are thinking. As long as we remain wholly on the Physical plane of consciousness this process goes on under the Law of Instinct both as to our bodies and our environment.

The natural Law of this plane of Instinct is an unconscious recognition—an automatic manifestation—of our *oneness* with all life, and so we do not have "lack" or poverty in our bodies or environment. This is best illustrated in what we call the "uncivilized" tribes which used to predominate in the world, some of which are still in existence, although few remain in their former purely

" Physical " or Instinctive state of consciousness. They did not work and did not need to for the Law of their lives led them to be born into an environment where Nature furnished them with sufficient to eat and wear without work.

Those who continued to live entirely in the physical side of their lives became over-developed in it, were unable to understand or appreciate any of the other states of consciousness and so continued to re-embody in a purely physical environment. We only need to study *all kinds* of people all over the world to be convinced of this truth.

As man went on in his evolutionary growth and unfoldment he began to use his physical brain—to think thoughts, to imagine or image things—and in this way he began to grow and develop his intellect. The more intellectual he grew, or as we call it the more " civilized " he became, the less instinctive he was, because, unconsciously to him, his intellect—his thoughts—dominated and controlled his " instinct "—the intelligence or mind of the cells of his body and environment—and they, obeying his " intellect," were deprived of their own initiative and the harmonious relationship which was *natural* to them, and he consequently attracted to his body and environment only such atoms as vibrated harmoniously with the thoughts he generated with the new faculty—his intellect.

To know the truth of this we only need to go back to the Indian of our own country and the frontiersman who, living largely in the instinctive side of their consciousness, could follow the trail of man or beast through pathless forests and could tell all about the person or animal they were following; when one who had developed his intellect and was living in that side of his life could not see anything to indicate the trail or that the forest had ever been penetrated before.

Some few men learned to combine their "instinct" and "intellect" and use the latter in further developing the former, and in all such cases they preserved their union—their *oneness*—with the Universal Life and knew no lack either in their body or environment.

The masses, however, unconsciously used their intellect to separate them from the One-Life, through the thoughts they generated and allowed to persist. They related in their thought world with the currents where lack, disease, fear, worry,

anger, hatred, envy, jealousy, strife, resentment, resistance, impatience, intolerance, condemnation, criticism, and kin-
dred thoughts found their home, and the
more often they related with these currents the more did they attract to themselves, both in body and environment, the
atoms which would make another inharmonious physical home where these conditions could manifest in material form.

As the result of the over-development
of the "intellect" and the under-develop-
ment of the other faculties we find men
who are living in emaciated physical bodies, devoid of all sense of instinct, inspiration, intuition, and revelation, but with
an intellect that in its "reason and
logic" is tremendous, but entirely in-
capable of appreciating the instinct of
the physical man, the inspiration of the

dreamer, the intuition of the mystic, or
the wonderful revelations which comes to
one who harmoniously combines and de-
velops all of these faculties. Such persons
have not yet learned that the true function of "logic" is to teach us the constructive use of our reason or intellectual
powers along harmonious lines.

These two states of consciousness, the
Physical and Mental, deal solely with the
states which have their initiative or origin in the physical body. When the physical body is destroyed by "death" these
two states of consciousness cease to manifest; that is the Mental state ceases to
manifest as soon as "death" ensues, and
the Physical state—the intelligence in the
cells of the body, the "sub-conscious
mind"—at once goes to work to disinte-
grate the body and upon the completion

of this it ceases to manifest in physical form. These two states of consciousness must have the objective body through which to manifest, otherwise their expression here on the material plane is impossible.

The other states of consciousness—the Soul or Inspirational, the Spiritual or Intuitional and Revelational—can manifest as well outside of the physical body as through it. It is true that in order for us to perceive the effects of their manifestations with our physical senses they must have a physical body of some kind through which to manifest, but they are separate and distinct from it and manifest through it rather than in it.

These states of consciousness are not under the dominion nor control of the Physical or Mental minds, neither do

they in turn control the mentality in any
way. The Physical mind—the cell consciousness or sub-conscious mind—is the
only mind or intelligence which is under
the control of the Mental mind or Intellect. The term "cell consciousness," as
used here, includes not only the intelligence in the atoms or cells of the physical
body but also that in the atoms of which
the environment is composed. These are
all under the control and domination of
the Intellect or Mental mind.

While it is true that the Soul and Spiritual minds or states of consciousness are
not in any way under the control of the
Intellect, yet the latter can make conditions both in the physical body through
which it is expressing and in the environment through which the Soul and Spiritual states of consciousness may express,

and this is one of the true and constructive functions of the Intellect.

Through the Soul state of consciousness we derive all of our great wonderful inspirations which increase our vibrations and when this is accomplished under the intelligent direction of our intellect we attract to us the more harmonious and constructive material with which we rebuild our physical bodies and their environment.

Our Intellect should direct us to such places where we will get this inspiration. We may obtain it in many different ways; through association with those persons who have already developed it, through hearing lectures, reading books, visiting art galleries, going to theatres which produce plays that inspire, through viewing a beautiful sunset, through thinking of the wonderful power manifested by Nature in the raising of the lofty, snow clad peaks of the Rocky Mountains, or the never ending flow and ebb of the tides at the seashore, through the gigantic waves that the monster Ocean Liners ride so easily, and through the wonderful mechanism of the human body. All these inspire us with the wonder and greatness of existence, and when our Intellect permits us to revel in their inspiration it raises our vibrations and makes us just that much stronger and more powerful.

But when our Intellect refuses to allow us to revel in the inspiration which these and other wonderful things give us, when it belittles the creative power of the God-consciousnss which manifests in all things, including man, when it places any kind of a limitation upon man's possibilities, then the vibrations of our atoms are slowed down and we draw from the formless energy everywhere around us only such atoms as vibrate at this slower rate, and it is in these currents where lack of all kinds is to be found.

The Spiritual state of consciousness is the vibration through which our intuition and revelation manifests. This is the vibration in which we get the real, the genuine, true-blue " hunches " of life. This is also the plane of consciousness from which our imagination obtains its most constructive and harmonious images.

The Imagination is a faculty which may be used by all of these different states of consciousness. Through its use we create everything we have both in body and environment, and the plane or state of consciousness from which we use it determines the kind and quality of the thing created. This most wonderful statement must be considered carefully in order to understand its stupendous import.

Many times people mistake an "impression" for an "intuition" and when the result proves different from what they expected they blame it on their "intuition," when, as a matter of fact, they themselves were to blame for not being able to differentiate between their "impression" and "intuition."

"Intuitions" never have their origin from anything on the objective plane, they always come from within, and are the result of our having, momentarily only perhaps, raised our physical vibrations to a point where this state of consciousness can manifest through the physical brain. Many persons do this frequently and un-

consciously; they do not know how they do
it and often do not know that they have
done it, and then their Intellect steps in
and tells them that such a thought was
"all foolishness" and so they pay no attention to it. Afterward they frequently
see their mistake and then they are wont
to say "Had my foresight only been as
good as my hindsight," etc. When we
touch this state of consciousness and
know it, and then follow the leading of
our intuition we never go astray, for it is
our highest state of consciousness trying
to manifest through us and by continually
listening to and following its instructions
we develop it more and more.

Our Intellect was given us for the purpose of taking our intuitions and revelations and working them out intelligently
in material form on the physical plane.

Can we imagine any more insane intuition, before it was materialized, than the reproduction of the human voice by machinery after the speaker is dead? Had not Edison by the intelligent use of his intellect worked out this dream into material form the phonograph would still be unknown. Without the Intellect to do this our intuitions and revelations would be as valueless to us on the physical plane as is an automobile without a chauffeur. The motor car, with an intelligent driver, can be made a most useful thing both for business and pleasure, and so with our inspirations, intuitions and revelations. That is why we should develop the Intellect, but it should be done intelligently and in a way that will enable us to use *all* of our faculties, Instinct, Inspiration, Intuition, and Revelation, as well as Mental, and not only some one or two of them.

"Impressions" have their origin solely in the objective side of life. They come as the result of the things we have learned on the objective plane through our physical senses. We may have learned them years ago, and perhaps forgotten, but they are stored up in the Intellect—the Mental mind—and come to us from that source. Having their origin in the objective world it depends on the basis or foundation on which they were originally built as to their value. "Impressions" are never safe to follow blindly because of the difficulty in determining their origin. It is interesting and instructive, sometimes, to follow them and see where they lead us. Many times this is the only way by which we learn to differentiate between them and our intuition.

CHAPTER III.

Man Has the Power to Develop Every State
of Consciousness.—How to Correct Too
Emotional Natures; also Those that are
Afraid.—The Faculties Used by the Successful Man.—What the Law of Force Is
and its Effects.—What the Law of Harmonious Attraction Is and its Effects.

We all possess within us the power to
unfold and develop, to the greatest per-
fection, every state of consciousness; in
fact most of mankind manifest them all in
some degree.

We have persons who are over-developed in some one of these different states
and under-developed in the others; these
find it difficult to express rationally, or
understand anything which is not directly
related to or connected with their own

particular state of consciousness or
unfoldment. Thus those who live continuously in the Inspirational, Intuitional
or Revelational states—these are more
generally known as the emotional states—
to the exclusion of the Instinctive and Intellectual states, become so abnormal to
the majority of mankind that they are
called insane. They are the " Col. Mulberry
Sellers " of the financial world, having
great, wonderful inspiration and oft-times
intuition and revelation as well, but lacking the intellectual development which
would enable them to materialize their
wonderful visions in a practical way on
the objective plane.

On the other hand we have people who
are over-developed intellectually; their
Intellect has made them as hard as flint;
they are what the world calls " practical "

men; their Intellect is always in absolute
control of every vibration; they would not
permit of an increased heart beat nor allow themselves to be thrilled with an inspiration for anything; they pride themselves upon having absolute control of
their "emotions" and would not allow
any such a "weakness" to manifest in
their lives; "An emotional nature is all
right for women and children," they say,
"but not for a man with red blood in his
veins."

Such lives have yet to learn that it is
not the emotional natures which are destructive any more than the mental, but
it is the use to which we put such natures,
such states of consciousness, which makes
them constructive and successful or destructive and unsuccessful.

The successful business man is one who

has some development of his inspirational and intuitional faculties but who guides and directs (instead of repressing) their manifestations with an intelligent application of his intellect.

When we live in any one of these states of consciousness to the exclusion of the others we can only relate with the things which are in its currents. We obtain such things under the Laws which prevail and control in that state of consciousness, and we can only retain them under the same Laws. But when we develop ourselves and learn to express in all of these states of consciousness, joining them all together in one harmonious expression, we learn to get what we want, get it when we want it, and keep it as long as we want it.

The Law under which we work in the Physical and Mental states of consciousness is the Law of Force. On the Physical plane this Law is expressed purely as brute force; whoever is the strongest, physically, is the most successful in this state of consciousness whether he be man or animal. On the Mental plane the expression of the Law of Force is more refined. In this state of consciousness men *make* others do their bidding through the developing and controlling of physical force by the intellect. The prize fighter or wrestler who has only physical strength stands no show whatever with the man who, even though of less physical strength, has developed his intellect and learned how to unite it harmoniously with his physical; while the machine—the product of man's intellect—can do the work of a hundred physical men and do it far better. In the world of business and finance the same truth prevails, and the man who has the sharpest and most developed intellect is the one man who has the greatest force in the purely Intellectual state of consciousness.

The Law which prevails in the Soul and Spiritual states of consciousness is the Law of Harmonious Attraction, the Law of Love.

This is a most wonderful Law although the words which symbolize it seem so simple. They are simple to us only because we have seldom or never seen beneath their purely intellectual interpretation. When we open ourselves to the inspiration of this Law of Harmonious Attraction and begin to study its operation by Nature we see that it is really the only Law which Nature, or God, uses throughout the universe.

The earth is held to its orbit in its journey around the sun through this wonderful Law of Harmonious Attraction. The sun throws out its great, beautiful love nature into space and entwines its arms around old Mother Earth, bringing life and vitality with every vibration, while the earth nestles and cuddles in the arms of the sun, evolving and developing the life within and upon it in this loving embrace.

The moon in its orbit around the earth is held under this same Law of Harmonious Attraction, and all mankind together with the things in all other kingdoms are held in the arms of old Mother Earth under this same Law of Love or Harmonious Attraction.

The seed when planted in the **ground**, under the same Law of Harmonious Attraction, sends its tiny rootlet down into the earth in order that it may be sure of a permanent supply of moisture, and its stem peeps out from under the clods, attracted there from the negative forces which surround it, in order to obtain the sunshine and rains and dews which are so necessary to its life and development.

Everywhere we look we can see some manifestation of this Law of Harmonious Attraction in Nature.

CHAPTER IV

How Most Persons Have Gained Success.—
Why It Has Not Been Permanent in Most
Cases.—How Man in His Scramble for
Money Resembles Chickens When They
are Fed.—People and Things are Instru-
ments in the Hands of God, the Great
Universal Law.—Why Methods do not Af-
fect One's Ability to Obtain Wealth
But Do Affect the Ability to Retain It.—
"Vacant Space" Filled with the One
Universal Substance.—"A Million Dol-
lars from Out a Blue Sky."—We Retain
Things under Same Law We Obtain Them.
—Wall Street Man's Experience.

The world has not had held before it
many shining examples of success, financial or otherwise, by those who have obtained it under this Law of Harmonious
Attraction. The success achieved by man
has been largely the result of the use of

the Law of Force, (and that is why it has not been permanent in most cases), through the intellectual and instinctive states of consciousness, and the world has therefore believed that the Law of Force was the real law of success.

The masses are like a lot of sheep and borrow their behavior from the few. In the matter of getting money they are like chickens about to be fed. A pan of food is placed in the center of the chicken-yard and the chickens come running toward it from all directions; the half dozen which reach it first grab something and start off on a run; the rest of the chickens, instead of going to the pan where the source of supply is and where there is an abundance of the food they want, run pell-mell, helter-skelter after the few chickens that have carried away with them only a small portion of the abundance of supply. The masses, like the chickens, instead of going to the source of the abundance of supply and creating something for themselves from out the formless energy, spend their time running after the few who have related with abundance and who have money, and in devising schemes to relieve them of it, never once realizing that people and things are only instruments in the hands of God—the great Universal Law—to give to us just what we have created for ourselves and that it is impossible for them to give us anything else. We see the truth of this manifested many times when we try to help others but cannot do so. Something always intervenes and prevents it.

The *methods* we use do not affect our ability to obtain wealth or success temporarily but they do affect our ability to retain them permanently.

The world has not yet come into a realization that everywhere around us in this "vacant space," as we call it, there is a live, vital, seething mass of energy, far more vital and powerful than anything man has yet harnessed in material form, and to which he may go and draw from it an eternal abundance of everything he wants.

While it is true this vital substance is invisible to the physical sight yet it is none the less true that it exists, just as the electric fan revolving at a speed so rapid we cannot see it, yet when the current is shut off and the vibrations of the fan lowered it begins to materialize and we can see it then with our physical eyes.

So with this invisible substance, when

we relate with it constantly and persistently in our consciousness in accordance with the image we have built and hold in our imagination we set up a strong, powerful vibration with our thoughts, and under the Law of Harmonious Attraction the atoms of this invisible substance with which we relate in our thought world begin to lower their vibrations and finally become materialized in form around us.

There is only one substance in the universe, and it is from this one substance that everything which we have ever materialized in form on the objective plane has been derived. This one substance may be differentiated into the myriads of material things we have had in the past, have now, or which we may create in the future, the differentiation being occasioned by the difference in the rate at which the atoms, composing the material form, vibrate.

When we understand this truth and use our Intuition to create as limitless a vision as we can of the thing we want, our Inspiration to increase our own bodily vibrations and relate us with the more rapid vibrating currents on the unseen side of life, and our Intellect to hold fast to this vision and inspiration, we have then effected a combination which, with these faculties working together in perfect harmony, will be able to reach out into the formless energy and attract the gold of the universe to us and differentiate it into form any time we may desire.

Now do not misunderstand me and get the idea that I either believe or teach that in our present state of consciousness it would be possible for any of us to sit with folded hands, with a blank, negative state of consciousness, and have a few million dollars drop into our laps from out the blue sky.

What I do mean is this: That through the operation of this Law of Harmonious Attraction we can make ourselves so full of the attractive power that over perfectly normal lines of transference on the objective plane, and in perfectly legitimate ways, old lines of transference will be increased, new ones opened up, and our earning capacity be increased way beyond what we have heretofore thought possible, and all this because people will *want* and love to do business with us rather than with those who try to *make* them through the use of the inharmonious Law of Force.

Under the Law of Force we are never sure of being able to retain what we do get. There is always the fear that we may make some unsafe investment, or that we will have something stolen from us, or that some one stronger and more powerful than we, or some one sharper, smarter, and less honest than we are will take it away from us, or that we will lose it in some way, or that whatever we do will be the " wrong " thing to do instead of the " right." This fear is well founded too, because we can only retain a thing under the same Law we obtained it. When we live under the Law of Force we always find some one, sometime and somewhere, who is able to use this Law more effectively than we can, and what we have obtained under it begins to leave us.

A Wall Street man once came to me with this story: He wanted to buy a property in New York. The price and terms had been satisfactorily agreed upon by both parties but the agent who was conducting the sale wanted the owner to pay him a larger commission than agreed. This the owner refused to do and the purchaser's contract expiring in the meantime the owner immediately sold the property to another party at a big advance in price.

This man did not learn, until it was too late, why his agent had not completed the sale. He had lived under the Law of Force all his life and so the Universal Law gave him what he had created for himself and took away, at the very last minute, this opportunity to make money, "through no fault of his" he and the world both said.

Later on this same man leased a property for hotel purposes and engaged another party to manage it. Through a combination of circumstances and conditions,

made possible only through the inharmony he had created under the Law of
Force, his Manager surreptitiously obtained a new lease in his own name and
ousted the employer from possession.

This same man owned a property in
process of development for which he was
offered and refused $300,000 cash. Later
on, through the men who managed the
corporation but who only held enough
stock by his permission to qualify as offi-
cers, he was sold out and only realized
about $40,000 from the wreck.

"Luck" you say! Well, "luck" is only
the *effect* of the energy we create in consciousness and it is for each and every one
of us to say whether this *effect* shall be
"good" or "bad luck."

Under the "Law of Harmonious Attraction" it is always "good luck" and

remains so.   Under the " Law of Force " as long as the *force* we use is stronger than that used by others we have " good luck " temporarily, but the fear that we will lose what we have is well grounded, for some day we run up against some one who uses the " Law of Force " better than we and our money melts away like dew before the morning sun.

These are only a few of the many negative registrations of the Law of Force in this man's life.   For four years prior to coming to me this man had been having a " hand to mouth " existence and had about completely lost his courage.

He was under my care and instruction for nearly a year and in that time financed one big deal and got two other large ones under way, aggregating considerably more than the first one, and so far his profits have brought him a quarter of a million dollars.

All this came to him under the Law of Harmonious Attraction and through his consciously building for it under this Law. He ceased to fight for anything, knowing, as he looked back over his life, that resistance and resentment create an energy which is always destructive and that it is far better to let go of everything which can be held only under the "Law of Force" and use the energy toward creating something else under the "Law of Harmonious Attraction."

Under this Law of Harmonious Attraction all fear disappears, for we know that this Law is stronger and more powerful than is the Law of Force, and that it is impossible for any one working under the Law of Force to take anything away from us unless we first create the destructive energy in our own consciousness which permits the Universal Law to use them as such destructive instrument in our lives, and that those who are working under the Law of Harmonious Attraction will not *want* to take anything away from us. We know that what we have created for ourselves under the Law of Harmonious Attraction is our own, for it came to us harmoniously and constructively and because the "other fellow" *wanted* us to have it and so we can keep it as long as we want it.

CHAPTER V.

Most Rich Persons are Young Souls; have had but Few Incarnations.—Ignorant Use of Intellect Separates us from Abundance of Supply.—How Wealthy Persons Set Causes in Motion in One Incarnation which Relates Them with Poverty in the Next.—"Like Produces Like" on Every Plane of Consciousness.—Intellect the Governing Power in Material World.—Mental Imbeciles.—Soul and Spiritual Imbeciles.—The Two Brain Centers: Physical and Psychological.

In analyzing these several states of consciousness it can readily be seen that one working on the Physical, or plane of Instinct, not yet having separated himself in his thought world from the abundance of supply is therefore still unconsciously related with it.

The majority of rich persons in the

United States are still comparatively young souls, that is souls or egos who have not had many incarnations. They are living largely upon the plane of In-stinct, and while they have Intellect and are usually very cultured, yet the fact that they have had but few incarnations in the physical body and have therefore not had the opportunity to create very much negative energy with their Intellect accounts for their not yet having set suffi-cient causes in motion to separate them from the abundance of supply.

There are some rich persons who are old souls and who are rich because they, either consciously or unconsciously, live under the Law of Harmonious Attraction most of the time; it is *natural* to them be-cause they acquired the *habit* in former incarnations.

As we go on in our growth and unfoldment, incarnation after incarnation, the
majority of us set negative, destructive
causes in motion, through our Intellect,
which separates us not only in consciousness but in the objective world from this
abundance of supply.

Many of the very poor persons we have
are those egos which, having lived
through the plane of Instinct and developed a sense of the plane of Intellect, but
not a sense of their responsibilities, have
accumulated such a vast amount of destructive energy as to make it necessary
for them to work it out through the poverty plane of consciousness.

It frequently occurs that lives which
have had every whim, every wish, every
desire satisfied in one incarnation become
so satiated with money from the over-

abundance of supply which they have had, that through their very satiety they set causes in motion which in their next incarnation relates them with the direst kind of poverty.

A woman once had a beautiful wrap presented to her and was going into ecstacies in her delight with it when another woman said, "Oh! could I only find something which would give me the joy that wrap gives to that woman."

The latter woman had had an overabundance of supply all her life, having been born into an inheritance of wealth and never having expressed a desire, which money could purchase, without having it satisfied. She had become satiated with wealth and did not recognize that in the energy which she had put into her statement and in the consciousness back of her words she was setting causes in motion which, with that same state of consciousness continued and persisted in, could only have the effect some day, either in this or some future incarnation, of relating her with poverty.

Now what is the value of knowing and understanding these different planes of consciousness? Simply this: that "like produces like" and "like attracts like" on every plane of consciousness and in every rate of vibration throughout the entire universe, and that when we know the kind of causes we set in motion—the kind of energy we generate—we also know the kind of effects which will result.

The object of life is to join all of these states of consciousness together, make union with and live in them all harmoniously at one and the same time.

Our fixed point of contact with the world, that is the state of consciousness with which we contact it and the things on the objective plane, must necessarily be from only one of these planes of consciousness. One of them predominates until we reach a perfected state of development, an evolutionary unfoldment, which enables us to blend them all into one harmonious whole.

The state of consciousness which predominates in our lives determines our vibration, and the vibration in turn determines the currents in this formless energy everywhere around us with which we relate and the kind of atoms we draw from it to our bodies and environment.

The Mental plane, or the plane of Intellect, is the plane of consciousness which should predominate in the objective world,

for it is only in this state of consciousness,
acting through the physical body, that we
are able to manifest on the objective
plane. Should man's physical brain—the
cerebro-spinal brain through which his Intellect operates—become atrophied from
disuse or seriously impaired through in-
jury, he becomes what we call an imbecile,
his five physical senses are destroyed, his
physical manifestations being only such
as come from the instinct or intelligence
in the physical cells of the body. On the
other hand, when his solar-plexus—the
psychological brain through which his inspirations, intuitions and revelations are
conveyed to him—becomes atrophied from
disuse or in any way seriously impaired
through the improper use or the ignorant
and destructive control of its functions
by the Intellect, he becomes just as much

of an imbecile on these higher planes of consciousness as he is on the Physical and Mental planes when his physical brain is impaired.

The world is full of soul imbeciles who cannot, in their present state of unfold-ment, either understand or comprehend these larger truths. It is impossible to "prove" the existence of a tree or any other material object to one who is a mental imbecile, because the faculties by which such object can be discerned are undeveloped. And so with the "soul im-beciles;" their intellects may be gigantic but their faculties by which these larger truths may be perceived and understood are undeveloped. "Soul imbeciles" some-times have great knowledge and wisdom but they always lack understanding. But no matter how atrophied their higher faculties may be they can be developed, and the human race as a whole is developing and unfolding them rapidly and therein lies our promise of the great future opening up before each one of us.

CHAPTER VI.

INTELLIGENT USE OF INTELLECT.—PHYSICAL AND
INTELLECTUAL GIANTS; SOUL AND SPIRITUAL
PIGMIES.—GOD GAVE US ALL POWER AND THE
FACULTIES THROUGH WHICH TO USE IT.—MAN
IS FREE TO USE THIS POWER IN ANY WAY HE
WISHES.—NO ONE HAS EVER ENSLAVED US BUT
OURSELVES.—UNIVERSAL ENERGY IS NEITHER
"GOOD" NOR "BAD."—MAN CAN USE IT TO
CREATE SUCCESS OR FAILURE, ABUNDANCE OR
LACK.—HOW MAN RELATES WITH THE LAW OF
FORCE.—HOW TO DISPLACE THE LAW OF FORCE.
—HOW TO "TURN ON THE LIGHT."—DOWN
BROADWAY TO THE BATTERY.

Before we can manifest intelligently on
the Physical plane we must develop the Intellect and through its intelligent use
of all our faculties we are then fully
equipped and able to master the external
world and all its conditions. We can
therefore readily see how very important

the Mental or Intellectual state of consciousness is to us.

The masses have sensed this truth in a dim way, and so there has ever been the desire to cultivate the mind and improve the intellect.

In our hunger for intellectual development we have lost sight of the Soul or Inspirational, and Spiritual or Intuitional and Revelational unfoldment, and of the necessity for our growth along these lines keeping pace with our intellectual and physical attainments. The result could only be what it has been, viz.: a race of physical and intellectual giants, and soul and spiritual pigmies. Unintentionally and unconsciously we have used our Intellect to cover over and bury deeply the Soul and Spiritual states of consciousness. It is true we have tried to satisfy their

incessant calls by devoting a small portion of one day out of seven to religious
forms and ceremonies which in reality
have only been an excuse for our neglect-
ing their development the rest of the time
and has better enabled us to bury them
still more deeply rather than assist us in
their unfoldment.

In the beginning God gave us all power
and the faculties through which to use
it; He also gave us the power to use these
faculties in any way our desires might
lead us. God never used the Law of
Force in our lives; He never told us that
we *must*, or *must not*, do anything. His
hand has never been laid on our lives in
any way; we have been free agents all
down the ages past and gone and will continue to be free agents all along the ages
yet to come to express ourselves in accord-

ance with whatever causes we may set in motion. No one has ever enslaved us in any way but ourselves; no one ever set a cause in motion but ourselves for which we are in any way responsible; no one ever will set a cause in motion but ourselves for which we will ever be responsible.

In this material world our responsibility begins and ends in the Intellect, the Mental plane of consciousness. When we use our Intellect, consciously or unconsciously, to generate thoughts in the physical brain which in any way lower our vibrations or retard or repress our ability to express, we are using the Universal Energy destructively; on the other hand when we use our Intellect to generate thoughts in the physical brain which are harmonious and constructive, and so increase our vibrations and enable us to

relate with more harmonious and constructive currents on the unseen side of
life, we are using this Universal Energy
constructively.

The Universal Energy—this one substance which pervades the universe, this
One Life in all and through all—is neither
" good " nor " bad " in itself; it simply
IS. It is like fire which in itself is neither
constructive nor destructive; it is the *use*
of fire which determines its effect. When
we use fire constructively it runs the commerce of the world both on land and sea;
it heats our homes and our business places
and keeps us from freezing in the winter
time; it cooks our food, and in fact becomes one of the most beneficial agencies
known to man. When we permit fire to
get out from under our control and run
riot it destroys our commerce both on land

and sea; it destroys our homes and business places; it destroys our food, and it even destroys us, and so becomes one of the most devastating agencies known to man; but in itself it is neither " good " nor "bad."

And so with this Universal Energy. We can use it to materialize an abundance of supply for ourselves, or we can use it to create poverty and lack. God does not attempt to tell us *how we must use it* any more than He attempts to tell us how we must use the fire.

The question then is, "How shall we use our Intellect in order that we may build consciously for permanent success?"

One of the very first things to do is to displace in our consciousness every thought which will in any way relate us with this Law of Force; that is, all anger, hatred, worry, fear, envy, jealousy, impatience, intolerance, resentment, resistance, condemnation, criticism, etc., everything that creates the energy which relates us with this Law of Force. We should displace such thoughts with those of kindness, patience, tolerance, love (not simply the personal kind), peace, poise, harmony, etc., these generate a constructive energy and relate us with the currents wherein are contained the atoms which will produce in material form the harmonious and constructive things we want.

When we first attempt to train our minds to displace these old negative, destructive thoughts we find it necessary to continually and persistently affirm our *oneness* with the thing we want, no matter how far away from its materialization objectively we may seem to be. We must *fill* our thought world with the thought of the thing we want, displacing again and again the thoughts which come to us of the thing we do not want, and in accordance with our persistency in displacing them will we materialize the thing we do want soon or late.

Our work should be done without worry, fear, strain, effort, or tenseness of any kind. These old negative thoughts will come back again and again until we have formed the new habit of *filling* our thought world with the thoughts of the things that we want.

When night comes and everything turns from light to darkness, as it has done every night since the beginning of the world, we do not fret and fuss and fume and cry about it and say " Oh, what's

the use of trying to get rid of this darkness? I have tried it again and again but
I cannot get rid of it and there is no use of
trying any more," but we just take the
darkness as a matter of course and *turn
on the light*.

We should use our Intellect to do this
same thing in our thought world and no
matter how often thoughts of poverty,
lack and failure come to us, no matter
how often we look into our pockets and
find them empty, no matter how poor and
poverty stricken our environment may tell
us we are today, no matter how often we
have failed to succeed in the past, no matter how dark the future may seem to us
today, these are, one and all, like the
" darkness " which comes to us every
night and we should give them no more
attention than we give to the night's

darkness, but *"turn on the light"* by making strong powerful affirmations, such as "I have wealth *now*, I have an abundance of money *now*, I am wealth *now*, I am success *now*."

Should we start to go down Broadway from 100th Street to the Battery and turn off Broadway at 99th Street, wander around for a while but finally return to Broadway, continuing on to 98th Street, turning off again and wandering around awhile on that street but finally returning to Broadway and continuing our journey, we could turn off Broadway at every cross-street we came to and it would not affect our ultimately reaching the end of our journey did we return to Broadway and continue our journey down town every time we recognized that we had gotten off Broadway. Our turning into the side streets would only delay our arrival at the Battery, *not prevent it.*

So with these negative, destructive thoughts of lack, poverty, anger, hatred, etc., which come to us from time to time; they will not prevent our ultimate success, but only delay it a little, when we learn to recognize that they create a destructive energy and we continuously and persistently displace them with constructive thoughts and affirmations every time we recognize that they have returned to us.

The length of time it will take us to arrive at our journey's end, that is form the *new fixed habit* in our lives of thinking constructively, will depend upon how often we "get off Broadway" and how long we stay off it on these side streets, that is how often we relate with the negative currents and remain in them—in their darkness—before we begin to displace them with the constructive thoughts.

CHAPTER VII.

How to Obtain What We Want, When and Where We Want It.—What Having "the Faith of a Grain of Mustard Seed" Really Means.—What Makes a Thing "Natural" to Us.—Fixed Habits.

In order to obtain what we want, when and where we want it, we must continuously and persistently affirm our *oneness* with the thing we want. We must be like the "lily of the field which toils not, neither does it spin, but Solomon in all his glory was not arrayed like one of them." Side by side with the lily is the rose, the geranium, and other flowers, the weeds, the grass, perhaps many different kinds of vegetables are also growing in the garden near by; close at hand is the forest and the fruit orchard with their many different kinds of trees and varied fruits; all these are growing in the same ground, watered by the same rains and dews, kissed by the same sunshine, breathing the same air, and yet each draws to itself only the kind of material from earth and air, water, dew, and sunshine, which goes to make its particular kind. And side by side in this beautiful world of ours lives the man who has reached out into the formless energy and with his consciousness materialized the wealth of the universe, also the other man who has reached out into this same formless energy and materialized the lack and poverty. One has gathered the flowers, the other the weeds. Why?

We have always dismissed such questions with the answer—"Because it is *natural* to them." But what makes it *natural* to them? Jesus said that ".When ye have the faith of a grain of mustard seed, ye shall remove mountains." We have never fully realized just what this word "faith" really meant in this connection. We have never looked upon the mustard seed, the lily, and the other things outside of the kingdom of man, as having intelligence or mind, or manifesting "faith," because the quality of their intelligence or mind and the action thereof was so different from the quality and action of what we called intelligence or mind in man. But now, understanding these different planes of consciousness in which man manifests, we can begin to see and understand how the things of the lesser kingdoms, the mineral, vegetable, and animal, may also manifest on and become common to at least one of these planes of consciousness, viz., the Physical or Instinctive plane.

The intelligence or consciousness in the atoms of the lily, mustard seed, etc., operating under the Law of Harmonious Attraction, vibrating at a rate peculiar to themselves, send out their conscious call into this one formless energy and everywhere, both on the seen and the unseen side of life, those atoms which are attuned to such call—like the wireless telegraph instruments receiving messages—hear, understand and obey and come rushing to answer it. There is no doubt, no fear, no worry, no anxiety in the consciousness of the lily, the mustard seed, etc., but what this result will occur, and the call is sent out with the utmost faith *knowing* that it will be answered.

It makes no difference how strong the

call of the weed, the rose, the turnip, the
cabbage, the apple, the corn, and everything else may be, it does not disturb the
lily nor in anyway distract its attention
from its own call. The lily never throws
up its hands nor says "Oh, dear me!
There's no use of me trying to get any life
or sustenance where all these other things,
bigger and stronger and more powerful
than I, are calling for it;" it never says
that "the big trees"—the trusts of the
vegetable kingdom—"have gobbled up
everything and we little fellows do not
have any chance any more;" it never says,
"I have done this all my life and still I
am only a lily instead of a rose;" but
holding continuously and persistently to
the vision of the thing it wants to be, its
call goes out morning, noon, and night,
persistently and everlastingly for the

thing it wants, and in response to its call the tiny rootlet creeps down into the earth and the stem peeps up into the sunshine from out the clods, and little by little, day by day, does the thing for which it continuously calls materialize in form.

When we learn to have the faith of the mustard seed, the lily, etc., that is when we have established in our lives the *fixed habit* of *filling* our thought world with the thought, the vision, the image of the thing we want, then that thing will begin to materialize in form around us like the lily and the mustard seed materialize their conscious call.

This faith—this consciousness—can be developed in every life, and somewhere down the line of our cosmic journey we one and all will develop it. Some will succeed in doing so in this incarnation, perhaps

in a few days, a few weeks, or a few
months, while others may take many incarnations in which to develop it. It is
for each life to say how quickly the work
will be accomplished for itself.

CHAPTER VIII.

WHY THOSE WHO HAVE "FAITH" DO NOT SUC-
CEED.—WHY ONLY THE THINGS WE DO NOT
WANT MATERIALIZE FOR US.—HOW TO MA-
TERIALIZE THE THINGS WE DO WANT.—EX-
PERIENCE OF STENOGRAPHER.—EXPERIENCE OF
BUSINESS MAN WHO ATTRACTED NEARLY TEN
TIMES AS MUCH IN 60 DAYS UNDER THE LAW
OF HARMONY AS HE HAD IN SIX MONTHS PRE-
VIOUS UNDER LAW OF FORCE.

Every day we meet persons who, upon
being taught these things, will say that
they have all this great faith; that they
believe all these wonderful truths and
practice them, yet they do not achieve success. Why? In all such cases I have
found one of two things to be true, either
their understanding of faith was like that
of the old woman who prayed long and
earnestly one night that God might re-

move the high hill at the back of her house in order that she might have a better view; upon arising the next morning she looked out of the window and finding the hill still there exclaimed, "Just as I expected!"

Occasionally, however, we do find those who undoubtedly have the faith and belief, and practice them with great understanding, and yet do not succeed. In such cases I have always found that an interior inharmony existed. Sometimes it had existed for so long and the persons had gotten so used to it that at first they honestly denied its existence, but a deeper study into their conciousness told the story of their interior inharmony, through which they generated the negative energy that prevented them from materializing the thing they wanted.

I have had many cases of patients and students who were strong, powerful creators, but who had reached a period in their existence where it seemed impossible for them to materialize any of their constructive creations; they materialized their destructive ones fast enough, but their constructive creations seemed impossible of actualization.

An examination into the conciousness and habits of such persons showed that their work was done under more or less of a strain; that they were invariably anxious or tense, rarely ever relaxing, with the result that they generated an inharmonious energy, constructed an inharmonious wall around them in which they were enclosed like a shell; this prevented the things that they had created, and which stood just outside of this wall

or shell, from entering their atmosphere
and materializing in form. Just as soon
as this wall of inharmony could be dissi-
pated and dissolved, through treatments
for harmony, and the patients taught
how to relate with the harmonious currents through deep breathing and proper
affirmations, the things which had been
created before in their thought world began to materialize in form around them.

A woman came to me once who said
that for six months she had been answer-
ing an average of twenty advertisements
a week for a position as stenographer but
had failed to receive one reply to all her
applications. Just think of the kind of a
conciousness which could send out over
500 letters to people who wanted a stenographer (the kind of services she had to
give) but yet could not relate with one re-

ply, and was not even given an opportunity to demonstrate her ability. She
said that when she " sent out her answers
that she knew it would not do any good "
and then she added most convincingly,
" and it didn't."

Her trouble was that while she had
built a position for herself in her consciousness she did not know it and was
afraid to really believe in her own ability
to create for herself the thing she wanted;
there could only be one result from her
holding the image that " it would not do
any good " and she got that result.

I told her to continue doing exactly the
same thing she had been doing, viz.: answer the advertisements for " stenographer wanted," and to send out each
letter with the thought and affirmation
that *it* was *the* one which would connect

her with the position she had built for herself.

In less than one month she had six offers of a position and came to me to ask which one she should take. I told her to take which ever one appealed to her the most. She said the one she wanted did not pay as much as she desired. I told her to take it anyway as it was evident that was all the salary she had so far created for herself; that by taking it she was getting all she had attracted; that the position would give her work while she was creating a larger salary for herself in her consciousness. About three months afterwards she came to me and said that she was still at the same salary, and that she had been informed the position never had paid any more, so she would have to either *make* her employer pay her more

or get another position. I told her that
when she had created the increase in her
own conciousness and then " let go " so
the position could materialize that
either her employer would voluntarily
give her the increase or else some one
would offer her another position at the
increased salary she desired; that until
she did create it for herself in her own
consciousness she could not get *and hold*
such increase. I told her that every time
she thought of the question of salary she
should *see* herself—that is imagine or
image herself—drawing the salary she
desired and that in accordance with the
continuity and persistency with which
she did this would she materialize it. In
about a month she informed me that her
employer had voluntarily raised her salary to the amount she desired.

A man came to me one day and said that his business had been "rotten" for several months and that he had to raise $2,000 with which to pay some bills and back salaries of employees or go to the wall; that he had about $2,500 owing him for which he was going to sue the parties unless they paid at once.

I told him that unless he had created the money for himself in his own thought world it would be useless for him to sue as he would not get it, and that when he had created it in his thought world it would not be necessary for him to sue. I also said to him that there was plenty of money in the world, also plenty right here in New York, and there was no reason, except his own ignorance, why he should not relate with and attract to himself all he wanted or needed; that he could have

enough with which to pay all his bills and
more with which to carry on his business,
but that he would have to create it for
himself before he could get it. I told him
to FILL his imagination with the image,
the thought, the idea, that he had several
thousand dollars NOW; that he was free
from all financial worry and had all the
money NOW he needed or could use, and
to hold persistently to that image, and
every time the thought or image came
into his field of consciousness which in
any way dimmed or impaired that image
to at once displace it with the new image I
had given him. He had formed the habit
of imaging lack and that he was now to
change that habit and form the new one
of imaging abundance of supply and his
harmonious oneness with it; that as soon
as this new image had displaced his old

one he would materialize the abundance under the Law of Harmonious Attraction.

In less than one week he returned with this story: Upon leaving my office after the previous interview he had gone back to his place of business but had been there only a short time when an entire stranger came in and asked for an estimate on some work he wanted done. Upon returning for the estimate a few days afterwards my client was given the work which amounted to over $9,000 and also given an advance cash payment of $4,500 on account of the contract. In reporting the case my client said that in all his experience in the business covering some twenty years he never heard of anyone receiving a cash payment simply on an estimate and before any work had been done. This payment enabled my client to pay all his bills and left him with some ready cash as a working capital. As the result of following my instructions this man told me he took in over $20,000 in cash within sixty days from the time he first came to me although he had taken in less than $2,000 in the six months preceding that visit.

CHAPTER IX.

The Relationship Between the Thing Cre-
ated and the Energy which Created It.—
The Law of Cause and Effect.—How Each
Life May make the Affirmation "I Am
Success NOW" Become a Scientific and Ma-
terial Truth.—Why Continuously Think-
ing that "I Am a Failure" Makes Success
Impossible.—Story of the "Lunkhead."

The world has never understood the
relationship between the energy we generate with our intellect through the
thoughts which we permit to find lodgment in our physical brain, and the materialization of that energy in objective
form. The relationship between the real
cause and its materialized effect has been
hidden too deeply to be discerned by those
who lived only in their intellect to the exclusion of their other faculties.

The rich and purse-proud kings of finance seeing nothing but an abundance of supply in the world in which they live do not have a consciousness of poverty or lack but are like Marie Antoinette who when told that the people of France were starving because they had no bread asked, "Why don't they eat cake?" And they never do create such a consciousness until, through the accumulation of negative energy generated under the Law of Force through several incarnations of temporal power which their money gives to them, the time comes for them to reap the harvests of the causes they have set in motion, the seeds they have sown.

The masses, not knowing the Law of Cause and Effect—being ignorant of these truths and looking only on the objective side of life, seeing everywhere around them the physical expression of misery, poverty and lack—grow attached to the things of the senses and find it difficult to believe there is an abundance for them and that they can displace the image of lack and poverty—which they receive from this objective view—with one of opulence and abundance of supply such as the rich and wealthy have.   Their intellect has been educated only to the point which will permit them to believe in what they call "facts," that is, the things which have been materialized and which can be determined by their five physical senses. Not knowing the relationship between the energy generated by the intellect in the thought world, and the things—the facts —which they find materialized in form around them it is natural to believe these material things are the real facts.

But when we learn this great truth—viz., that before anything can be materialized in form it must first be created in consciousness and then worked out into form through the intellect—and then apply this truth, not only to some things but to all things, we can then begin to see how when we say "I am success NOW," not only once but thousands of times a day, FILL our field of consciousness—our thought world, our imagination—with this inspired thought, this intuitive affirmation, this wonderful vibration, as continuously and persistently as do the mustard seed and the lily, that only one result can accrue and that is we become success.

Many who have used the intellect to bury the soul and spiritual states of consciousness will say that we cannot affirm

"I am success NOW" when we "know
we are flat failures," for that would be
telling a lie. Of course we cannot under
such circumstances, for as long as we have
a consciousness that "we are failures,"
as long as we live in that thought and
"know we are failures," God Himself cannot help us, and we continue to be failures. But the moment we get even a little
glimmer of the light, the moment we begin to believe it is still possible that we
might achieve success, and then begin to
breathe deeply and affirm "I am success
NOW," just that moment do we begin
to relate with the success currents of the
universe and in accordance with our persistency and continuity in the affirming
of this new habit of thinking we are success NOW will we become successful.

One time a Vermont farmer was comparing himself to some of his old school-mates; he said: " I am the biggest lunk-head that ever was and I know it. Now there is Joe Lake who didn't know half as much as I did; he was a regular lunk-head but didn't know it and now he is a Railroad President. Then there was Bill Johnson whom I always had to help with his lessons; he was another lunk-head but didn't know it and now he is President of a big Bank. Then there was Sam Williams who was always at the foot of the class; he was another lunkhead but didn't know it and now he is President of the biggest Trust Company in the country. Then there was John Wilson, the fool of the class; he was another lunk-head and didn't know it and now he is worth millions and at the head of some of the biggest corporations in the country.

I was a lunkhead too, but the trouble with me was that I knew it and so I am still here on this rocky old farm."

The above homely story tells the law of success and of failure in a few words. We must never get the image that we are a "lunkhead" unless we want to be a failure. God—the great Universal Law—manipulates people and things in accordance with the image we hold continuously and persistently in our imagination.

CHAPTER X.

Every Material Thing is the Objective Symbol of the Vibratory Rate of the Atoms which Compose it.—How to Demonstrate the Difference in the Vibration of Words. —How We Relate with Failure.—How to Turn Failure into Success.—Story of the Artist.—How Negative, Destructive Energy is Generated Unconsciously.—How to Displace it.—The Law of Life.

It is a well established scientific fact that every material thing is but the objective symbol of the vibratory rate of the atoms which compose it; that the reason there are no two persons just exactly alike, and no two things of any kind anywhere which are exactly alike, is because of the difference in the rate at which their atoms vibrate.

The reason "a" is "a" and not the

letter "b" is because they are both objective symbols of different vibratory
rates.   Did they both symbolize exactly
the same rates of vibration, motion or
action, we would need but the one symbol.
What is true of letters is also true of a
combination of letters or words, and what
is true of words is also true of a combination of words or sentences.

Suppose we take the words "I am success" and repeat them as fast as we can
for five minutes, observing the vibrations
which they set up within us and the
thought currents with which they relate
us.   Then let us take the words "I am a
failure," and repeat them as fast as we
can for five minutes and observe the vibrations which are set up within us and the
thought currents with which they relate
us.   We need only to make this one sim-

ple little experiment to convince ourselves of the difference in the vibratory rates which words symbolize and their effect upon us when we establish the habit of living in their currents.

The words "I am success NOW" repeated once or twice, or only a few times, do not affect us materially, but when they are repeated continuously and persistently and as rapidly as we can speak them, so that all other thoughts will be displaced completely, they will relate us with a strong, powerful vibration which will bring strength, courage, ambition, and a belief that success *is* possible for us.

On the other hand when we live in the thought of "I am a failure" and make such thoughts the law of our lives it can readily be seen that we relate with the currents in which failure, loss, lack and all the misery which these things bring are to be found.

This truth is so stupendous, yet so simple and so subtle, that it is hard for us to realize it; in fact many persons do not know that we are living in the failure thought currents most of the time but believe we are living in thoughts of success, so subtle is the action,'and until we put our conscious mind on the thoughts we are thinking and learn through study the difference between constructive and destructive thoughts and their action it is hard for us to believe that we do have a failure consciousness. So strong is the habit of negative thinking in the mass mind that we have to watch persistently, continuously, intelligently and understandingly before we can displace it with the fixed habit of constructive thinking.

Should we go into the poor and poverty-stricken districts of any city in the world and interview the residents thereof we will occasionally find one who in the midst of his poverty-stricken environment says he knows he will be rich some day; not that he hopes he will but he *knows* he will. Should we follow up such lives we would find them gradually evolving out of the bondage of poverty into the freedom which comes with an abundance of supply.

When we are objectively poor but have a rich consciousness we can materialize wealth at once, but when we are poor both in our external expression and in our interior consciousness we must change the latter and develop a consciousness of the abundance of supply and our *oneness* with it before we can ever hope to materialize wealth and riches.

There was once an artist who was very poor. His studio was on the top floor of a tumbledown tenement and could only be reached by climbing half a dozen flights of ricketty stairs which endangered both life and limb every time they were scaled. When this man learned of the Law of Harmonious Attraction and the abundance of supply, and came into the conviction that it was possible for him to relate with it, he wrote the words "*I am wealth now,*" on large sheets of old wrapping paper and pinned them to the walls of his studio where they were constantly before him no matter which way he looked.

The few friends who visited him from time to time laughed at "his innocence, his foolishness," as they termed it, and in their "superior wisdom" they would exchange meaning glances, smile indulgently and tap their foreheads, saying, " Well I guess he is harmless anyway."

The artist let them have their fun while he went to work on what he determined would be his masterpiece, a picture which would bring him honor, fame, and wealth. Every time he mixed his paints he poured into their atoms the thought vibrations of " *I am wealth now.*" With every touch of his brush upon the canvas he breathed this thought. Surrounded on all sides by poverty and lack he concentrated all the power of his inspiration and intuition, under the direction of his intellect, on wealth and success, never permitting a thought of fear, failure, or lack to find lodgment in his field of consciousness, his imagination. Every time such thought would try to gain entrance therein he closed his eyes and dreamed the dreams of wonderful wealth and success which his inspiration and intuition brought to him and then, living in that consciousness, in the wonderful, glorious, beautiful, harmonious vibrations which he touched, he resumed his work of painting.

Finally the picture was finished and placed on exhibition. It was a masterpiece in the world of art and brought fame and honor to the artist, and in a short time was sold at an almost fabulous price, thus materializing his conscious creation of wealth made in the midst of an environment of poverty.

Many persons say "Why I never had the slightest fear but what I would succeed and yet failure came to me. Why was it?" This is an experience which comes to some lives. The reason for it is simply this: Such persons generate the negative energy, which embodies in form as loss of money or lack of success, through thinking thoughts of anger, hatred, worry, fear, anxiety, impatience, intolerance, condemnation, criticism, envy, jealousy, strife, resentment, resistance, etc., and by being tense and repressing their energy. All these emotions generate a negative, destructive energy which must embody in form unless it is antidoted or displaced. The physical body and environment afford the only two places where this energy can so embody and when the time comes for its materialization it seeks out the lines of least resistance. Should this be the environment then we have loss of money, position, friends, family, etc., lack of success in whatever we may be doing, or some of the many irritations which come to us in our daily lives, the degree of registration depending on the amount of energy generated and materializing at that particular time. In this way do we have loss and lack of success without ever having either imaged or feared it.

When we find ourselves caught in any of these negative states of consciousness, instead of repressing the energy, we should displace the destructive thought or image with a constructive one and allow the energy to express along harmonious lines. Thus by displacing any of these thoughts or images, such as anger, etc., with the thought and image of "All is good," *filling* the imagination with this idea, saying it over as fast as we can and continuing to say it until we are carried by its vibrations out into the thought currents with which it relates us, we then express this energy constructively and are benefited by its expression instead of being torn to pieces by its expression as anger, or through its repression, both of which are highly destructive.

The Law of Life is Expression; the Law of Death is Repression; we should live to express but learn to express harmoniously and constructively.

CHAPTER XI.

How to Build a Success Consciousness.—A
Personal Experience.—Each Life has an
Inexhaustible Supply of Constructive En-
ergy Upon which it May Draw.—How We
May Relate with It.—Our Attitude to-
wards Things Governs their Effect on Us.
—What Our Attitude Should be Toward a
Thief or Other Destructive Instrument.—
"Children in Consciousness."—Defense is
Neither Offense nor Attack.

How may we build a consciousness by
which we can materialize money and success? This is a question in which we are
all interested and which we will all learn
to solve somewhere down the line of our
cosmic journey.

There is only one sure, certain and
never-failing way and that is, first, last
and all the time to *live in and affirm our*

oneness NOW with the currents which make for wealth, success and harmony.

We do this by affirming "I am wealth NOW," "I am success NOW," "I am harmony NOW;" *filling* our thought world—our imagination, our field of consciousness—with these thoughts, displacing again and again all thoughts of failure, lack, inharmony, etc., until we have established the *fixed habit* of living in and breathing these constructive thoughts, until we do this unconsciously, do it because it has become *natural* to us.

Several years ago I began to establish the habit of concentrating upon the thought of health, wealth, and harmony as I walked to and from my office. I determined to build a consciousness of my *oneness* with these things and build it so strongly and powerfully that every atom of my body and environment would be so thoroughly impregnated with this thought and its image would be so deeply stamped thereon that the time would come when it would be impossible for me to attract even one atom to either my body or environment which did not vibrate in perfect harmony with these three conditions.

At first I had to put my conscious mind upon my thought world every time I started out to walk. Many times I would forget it entirely, again I would remember it only when I was near my journey's end, while frequently I remembered when I first started out.

No matter how often I forgot I kept persistently vowing that I never would forget it again with the result that to-day whenever I start to walk anywhere this habit has become so thoroughly *fixed* in my life that unconsciously and naturally, as the result of the habit, I begin to concentrate upon health, wealth, and harmony.

Slowly one by one the things which do not harmonize with these conditions are being sloughed off my life by the Universal Law and in their stead I am attracting the things which do harmonize with them.

All of us—young as well as old souls—have generated an inexhaustible supply of constructive energy in the past. It is stored up for us in the Universal Energy and we can relate with it at any time by continually and persistently realizing in our thought world that we have actually made the connection.

This accumulated energy may be likened unto an ocean of water on the physical plane the supply of which is limit.

less but which is all enclosed by dams or levees. Everywhere on all sides are little gates which, upon touching the proper button, may be opened and the water allowed to run along the channel into which it is directed. So this ocean of constructive energy which we have generated in the past may be drawn upon for anything we wish by touching, with our thought, the button which will raise the gate leading to the channel of wealth, of success, of harmony, or any other channel into which we may wish to direct this energy.

As long as we give power to the things of the objective plane we cannot say that the doing of certain things is " good " for every one, or that the doing of certain other things is " bad " for every one. There are some things that are more constructive in our lives than are others not because they are necessarily any better but because it is easier for us to take a more harmonious attitude toward them. It is therefore impossible for any teacher to lay down a law in the handling of *things* which is applicable to all persons under all conditions. This much we can say, however, that it is never the thing itself which is " good " or " bad," which brings joy or sorrow, success or failure, but it is the attitude we take toward the thing.

In order to gain success then we should take a harmonious and constructive attitude toward everything that comes and so keep ourselves perfectly harmonious, and in that way make of the thing simply a stepping-stone to our success.

What we permit ourselves to think about a thing is what controls our atti-

tude toward it. Thus, for instance, when
we permit ourselves to condemn a thing
because we say it is "bad," or condemn
some person for any cause whatever, that
is taking a destructive attitude toward
that thing or person and no matter how
just we may think our position in the case
may be we cannot relate with these negative, destructive currents in our thought
world and expect constructive and harmonious effects, any more than we can expect
to walk through a mud hole without getting mud on us.

A natural inquiry which would be made
right here by the masses is this: "Sup-
posing some one should steal our pocket-
book, are we to say *that* is 'good' and not
try to get it back or punish the thief
should he be caught?"

Remember again that it is never the

thing we do but it is the *way* we do it, *the consciousness back of the thing we do,* that makes it constructive or destructive. We always have a perfect right and it is always constructive to defend ourselves and our property but it is just as surely destructive for us to step over the line of defence and into the line of offence or attack. The line of demarcation between defence and offence is so slight and so subtle that it is difficult for the evolving soul to determine just where defence ends and offence begins. Like everything else, however, the beginning and ending are in the thought world, in our consciousness.

When we pursue a thief with the desire in our hearts to punish him, or when we attack some one in return in an attempt to "defend" ourselves from their attack, we are stepping over the boundary line of defence and are well into the vibrations of offence. When we condemn a thief, or any-one else, in our consciousness, no matter what they have done, we have again stepped over the line of defence and into that of offence. It is perfectly legitimate and constructive to analyze anything and everything as long as we do not criticize or condemn. Jesus said " I judge no man, neither doth my Father in Heaven (Father in Harmony) judge any man." He under-stood this Law of Harmony.

The man who sells " blue sky," knowing that it is only " blue sky," to an unsuspect-ing public in the belief on the part of the latter that they are buying well secured stocks or bonds, the man who sells cotton goods under the representation that it is all wool, the man who forecloses a mortgage because the owner of the property cannot pay it when due although he wants to pay it and would do so were it possible for him to earn the money, the man who breaks into our place of business or our home and takes away our valuables without our permission—are one and all in the same class in this respect, that is, they are all working under the Law of Force. It is the only law they have ever known and therefore the best thing they know how to do; they have not yet learned the Law of Harmonious Attraction, nor the destructive effects of the Law of Force.

It is true that the thief has learned that should he be caught he will undoubtedly be sent to prison. He does not fear to steal because it is wrong or destructive but only because he will be deprived of his liberty. The others, having nothing to fear in that respect—man-made laws being such as to protect them as far as prison sentences are concerned—go on under this Law of Force.

They are all simply children in consciousness—in their soul development and unfoldment. Were they two-year old children in physique and did these things we would not condemn them, so why, knowing that they are children in consciousness, no matter how old they may be in years as we measure time, should we condemn them? We should not. " Vengeance is mine, saith the Lord "—the Universal Law—" I will repay."

We know that under the Universal Law this is true. The Lord—the Universal Law—can only repay here on the objective plane through manipulating people and things, and so people and things become the instruments in the hands of the Lord—

the Universal Law—which He uses to work out in us the effects of the causes we alone have created and set in motion.

When we allow our consciousness to be filled with the desire to punish the thief who steals our pocket-book we put ourselves in the negative destructive currents where the Lord—the Universal Law—can manipulate and use us as a destructive instrument to give to the thief the destructive effects of the destructive causes with which he related when he took the pocket-book under the Law of Force. In becoming such a destructive instrument we, in turn, set destructive causes in motion the effects of which we will have to reap later on, and some one else, through the manipulation of the Universal Law, will be used as the destructive instrument to work out in our lives the effects of such causes.

Again it would be impossible for any one to steal anything from us had we not some time before that created in our thought world, through destructive and inharmonious thinking, the energy which when embodied in form related us with such a loss. This being the case we can readily see that we must cease generating and relating with such negative energy should we desire to stop having such losses and discontinue registering the destructive effects of the negative energy we have created in the past.

In defending ourselves objectively against such a loss we have a perfect right to pursue the thief, capture him when we can, and obtain the return of our property. We also have a right to protect ourselves and society from the acts of such "children in consciousness" during the time they are being taught to displace the Law of Force with the Law of Harmonious Attraction, and for this purpose Schools of Detention—not prisons—should be established where those who commit such overt acts may be detained while taught more, constructive methods.

In the meantime those on the outside of these Schools of Detention should also be taught this same truth to the end that mankind everywhere may cease to set these destructive causes in motion which relate us with the destructive effects.

CHAPTER XII.

PEOPLE ARE ALL IN DIFFERENT STATES OF UN-
FOLDMENT.—RECOGNITION DETERMINES WHAT
IS POSSIBLE OR IMPOSSIBLE FOR EACH LIFE.—
STORY OF THE STREET-CAR DRIVER.—MAN BE-
COMES A CONSCIOUS CREATOR.—HOW.—PEOPLE
OF THE UNITED STATES MORE EVENLY DE-
VELOPED.—UNITE THE IMAGINATION AND IN-
TELLECT MORE HARMONIOUSLY.—FIRST "BUILD
CASTLES IN THE AIR" BEFORE THEY CAN BE
BUILT ON THE GROUND.

We are all souls unfolding from different planes of consciousness, we are in
different states of development, and like
the child whose intellect is being trained
we must first learn the simple rules of
arithmetic before we are prepared to solve
the more difficult problems of geometry
and higher mathematics.

We have recognized that in our present

state of development and unfoldment it is impossible for us to get hold of and play with the moon and we therefore change our "want" rather than bewail the "fate" which keeps the moon away from us. Great wealth may be just as far away from us to-day, in our consciousness, as is the moon and so for the time being we change our "want" and use a lesser ideal towards which we find it less difficult to develop our consciousness.

We never lose sight of the greater ideal, but with the lesser one—the one which *seems possible* for us to accomplish *NOW*— we go steadily forward, developing our consciousness with the affirmation that we have this lesser thing *NOW* and we find that it does not take us long to materialize it objectively. This gives us greater faith and confidence in the power of our own creative ability and we increase our ideal and begin our work of mastering the new one; as fast as each new ideal is reached a still greater one comes into view, there being no limitation whatever to their greatness excepting such as we put on our inspiration, intuition and revelation with our intellect.

The following incident illustrates this truth.

Years ago, in one of our large and growing cities of the Middle West, a man was driving a street car at $1.10 a day.

In his dreams he saw himself in a policeman's uniform and, holding fast to that vision, in less than a year it was materialized.

He had no sooner donned the policeman's uniform than he dreamed another dream and saw himself passing step by step until he became a police captain and that dream was not long in materializing.

Still he was not satisfied but continued to build his " air-castles " and to live in his dreams; he saw himself in the position of Marshal of that county, a place which paid in fees over $50,000.00 a year, with a four-year term without re-election. By the intelligent use of his intellect it was not long before that dream in turn was materialized.

Having reached the pinnacle of success in official life, so far as money consideration for services was concerned, his dreams turned in another direction and he saw himself agent for a great public necessity having an exclusive control of its product, and this dream was materialized at the completion of his term as County Marshal.

Through the profits acquired by him in his progress in the development of his money consciousness he accumulated several million dollars, and to-day is the president and one of the principal owners of the street railway system in a city of nearly half a million population.

Had this man attempted to at once bridge the chasm between the street car driver at $1.10 a day and the millionaire owner of the street railway system he would have failed, but by putting aside his larger vision temporarily—although never losing sight of it—taking up and materializing these lesser visions, he was finally able to materialize the apparently impossible vision of his street car driver days.

During all his onward progress he used his intellect to hold fast to the dream vision which his inspiration, intuition and revelation brought him, doing that which he found nearest at hand to do with all his might and, as each new dream materialized, his inspirational, intuitional and revelational faculties unfolded to him the possibilities of still greater things to be accomplished, still larger things to be done, and God—the great Universal Law —manipulated people and things in the unfoldment of that life—as He does in every life—in accordance with the visions created and which are held continuously and persistently in the thought world by the intellect.

The lily of the field has limited itself to being a lily and as long as it remains in that state of consciousness it will continue to be a lily, reproducing itself again and again, but the day will come in its evolution and unfoldment when it will have a consciousness of something greater, something larger, something better, and it will then begin to evolve into this new and greater ideal.

So with man. In the physical state of consciousness we go on relating with and reproducing our kind until through our evolutionary growth we become intellectual. Before that time we are unconscious or instinctive creators, we are in our Garden of Eden, our Paradise, but *when we begin to use our intellectual faculty we become conscious creators and can create just what we may desire* and are held accountable under the Universal Law for the causes we set in motion—the energy we generate—by the use of this new faculty—the intellect. It is the inharmonious, ignorant and destructive use of the energy by our intellect **that drives us out of our " Garden of**

Eden" and causes us to lose our "Paradise."

What we create and the extent and quality of our creations are determined by the faculties we use. When man lived wholly on the plane of instinct and only used that faculty he lived like the beasts of the field and roamed the country without home, clothing, or any of the things which civilized man calls the essentials of life.

As he commenced to use his intellect and develop the intellectual state of consciousness he began to use fires with which to warm his body and cook his food, clothing to cover his nakedness, and huts in which to sleep.

As his inspiration, intuition and revelation began to express he dreamed of more pretentious places of habitation, finer,

better made and more comfortable gar-
ments to wear and, using his intellect intelligently, he realized and materialized
these dreams.

Had he not been inspired with the idea
of something better than the skin of
animals for clothing, and tents, caves and
huts for dwelling-places, and had not his
intuitive and revelational faculties told
him better things were possible, and had
he not developed his intellect to where he
could work out these dreams and visions
in material form, he would still be in his
instinctive state of consciousness and our
civilization would not yet have dawned.

In studying and analyzing the history
of the nations of the earth today it does
not require a very deep thinking student
to appreciate the fact that the people of
the United States as a whole, have de-

veloped these five faculties more evenly and made their combination more harmonious than have the people of any other nation on the face of the globe.

It has required a most wonderful inspiration with great intuition and revelation, backed up by a powerful intellect, to work out into objective form the mighty . buildings and the magnificent bridges, the great factories, the wonderful transportation facilities, the schools of learning, etc., which have been materialized here, and the colossal fortunes which have been accumulated in this country in the last half century.

The wonderful inventions of the past, such as the cotton gin, the sewing machine, the telegraph, the telephone, the phonograph, wireless telegraphy, the airships, the various kinds of farm machinery, machinery for making shoes, for making paper out of wood, for spinning cotton by which one man now does the work better and in less time than several dozen men used to do under the old methods, and those wonderful leviathans of the machinery world in use in digging the Panama Canal by which one machine in twelve minutes does the same amount of work which formerly took several hundred men several days to do, all these are the result of the great wonderful inspiration, the intuitive knowledge, and the master revelations their inventors had and which were worked out and materialized on the objective plane through the intelligent application of the intellect.

Some forty years ago Jules Verne, the noted French author, wrote three books entitled respectively " A Trip Around the

World in Eighty Days," "Twenty Thousand Leagues under the Sea," and "A Journey to the Moon." The world laughed and pooh-poohed and made fun of the great "crazy" imagination, as they called it, of Jules Verne and said that it was impossible to accomplish any one of these three things; but a trip around the world may now be made in less than forty days, and submarine boats are an accomplished and materialized fact.

Neither one would ever have been materialized had they not been built first in the consciousness—the thought world, the imagination, for that is where we do our imaging—of some mind through the power of its inspirational, intuitional and revelational faculties and then through the intelligent application of the intellect worked out into material form.

Some day the world will learn the great lesson that we must first " build castles in the air "—in the thought world, the imagination—before we can build them on the ground.

The object of calling attention to these things is that the world may see plainly the power of the inspirational, intuitional and revelational faculties when intelligently used by the intellect and how necessary it is for us to develop these faculties and learn how to use them constructively by the intellect. Without the combination working together harmoniously it is impossible to achieve great success along any line.

While we are developing and equalizing the development of these faculties in our own lives we may through a combination of individuals, each of whom has developed a different one of these faculties but all working together harmoniously toward the one great end, achieve wonderful success, but it is necessary to have all of these faculties in expression, either in a single person or in a combination of persons, in order to produce great success.

CHAPTER XIII.

THE FIRST THING NECESSARY IN BUILDING A
CONSCIOUSNESS OF MONEY.—THERE IS AN
ABUNDANCE OF MONEY IN THE WORLD.—
"CHANCE," "ACCIDENT," OR "LUCK" DOES NOT
ENTER INTO OUR SUPPLY.—WHY THE "OTHER
FELLOW" HAS MONEY AND WE HAVE NONE.—
HOW WE CAN RELATE WITH AND ATTRACT
MONEY TO US.—OUR PART OF THE WORK.—
GOD'S PART.—THE TRUE LAW OF SUCCESS.—
EXPERIENCE OF PHYSICIAN.

In the building of a consciousness for
money, the first thing is to realize that
there is an abundance of money in the
world NOW.

When we stop and think for a moment
we know that this statement is true.
Should we have any doubt about it all we
need to do is to visit the United States
Treasury, or some great banking institu-

tion, and see the vast piles of money which they have in storage.

We can also take a stroll on Broadway and visit some of the "Lobster Palaces" along "The Great White Way," or some of the fashionable hotels and restaurants on Fifth Avenue, and we will have no difficulty whatever in coming away perfectly satisfied that there is an abundance of money in the world.

How can we help being satisfied of this truth when we see the men in such places pull out of their pockets rolls of money big as two fists, containing nothing less than $100 bills which they keep for small change, most of their roll being composed of $500 and $1000 bills, and then see them give the waiter a $500 bill with which to pay for a dinner costing perhaps $150, telling the waiter to keep the change.

While we realize that this method of reckless, extravagant, prodigal expenditure is destructive, yet we cannot help but admire the opulent consciousness of these spenders in New York's gay life.

I hear some one say "Yes, there is plenty of money in the world but the other fellows have it all while I do not have any."

Why do the "other fellows" have all the money, and why is our supply so limited? This is not the result of "chance," "accident," or "luck;" it is the normal effect of a perfectly natural law which every life uses, either intelligently or ignorantly, consciously or unconsciously, constructively or destructively; the method of using this law by each life determines its effect on the environment.

Those who are rich have *recognized* their

oneness with the abundance of supply. They developed that recognition either in former incarnations and so were born into an environment of abundance in this one, or else they have developed it in this incarnation. When they developed it is immaterial in so far as the fact of their having developed it is concerned.

When we have lack it is because we have *recognized* our separation from this abundance of supply either in former incarnations and therefore were born into an environment of lack in this one, or else we have unconsciously and ignorantly developed that consciousness in this incarnation, for unless we had recognized in our consciousness our separation from the abundance of supply we never could have been separated from it on the material or objective plane.

The second step, therefore, is for us to begin to create a consciousness that it is possible for us here and now to relate with the abundance of supply just as well as anyone else.

The only way such a relationship can be established is through the people and things on the material plane, because the Universal Law can only manifest in objective form in the material world through them. Because of this fact many have obtained the idea that they must manipulate people and things in order to get the money but that is where we have made a big mistake.

While it is true that under the Law of Force we can and do manipulate people and things, just as the chickens run after and snatch the food from each other, and we can achieve temporary success and

obtain large fortunes as long as we exert
the stronger force, yet the time always
comes somewhere down the line of our
cosmic journey when some other life is
able to manipulate the Law of Force in a
stronger way than we and then our
fortunes begin to crumble and melt away.

· Under the Law of Harmonious Attraction the manipulation of people and things
belongs to God—the great Universal
Law—and is a part of the work with which
we have absolutely nothing to do. This is
a statement which will require careful
study and consideration in order to begin
to appreciate its great importance and
wonderful action.

Our business is first, last, and all the
time, through the power of our inspiration,
intuition and revelation, to create and fill
our imagination with this image and vision

of the abundance of supply and our *oneness*
with it, using our intellect with which to
hold it so strongly and powerfully that all
the poverty and lack of the objective plane
cannot dim it, and then go on with the
work in which we are now engaged on the
objective plane, like the street car driver
did, doing it with all the harmonious and
attractive soul energy we are able to generate, and permit God—the Universal Law
—to do the manipulating of people and
things.

When we do this we will find that one
by one new avenues, new and increased
lines of transference, will open up to us
and keep pace with our increasing development, just as they did in the street car
driver's case and many other similar ones.

The principle—the law under which God
works through man—is exactly the same

as it is under which He works through the other kingdoms. The lily gets the vision and then God—the great Universal Law—has man plant the seed, then water, cultivate, and take care of it. God—the Universal Law—can only manifest on the material plane through the people and things of this plane because there is nothing else here.

When we understand this truth and attend to our part of the work and let God attend to His, working together in perfect harmony, He does for man what He does for the lily, and the money, as well as everything else, which comes to us under this Law of Harmonious Attraction, comes to us because *it wants to come* and not because we make it come against its desire.

The true Law of Success is the Law of Harmonious Attraction. Many lives are unconsciously working under this Law most of the time. Sometimes they ignorantly and unconsciously live in the currents of the Law of Force for a while and then they wonder why "bad luck" comes to them. When living under the Law of Harmonious Attraction they belong to the class of people to which the world refers as being so "lucky" that they "could fall into the water without getting wet."

When such people get caught in the negative currents of the Law of Force they frequently do not know how to get out of them and then their condition is pitiable.

I was teaching a class in "Abundance" once in which there were several physicians and other professional men. One of the physicians told me the following story: He was a specialist and used to treat fifty or more patients a day; he had so much

work that it was necessary to employ
assistants. When he was going to his
office each day he always saw it filled, in
his imagination, with patients, and he always found them there on his arrival. One
day he was taken with a severe illness and
was kept from his work for several
months. During the time he was sick he
saw his patients scattered and his practice
dwindling to practically nothing. The
result was that when he was able to take
up his work again he had lost about all his
practice and although it had been three
years since that illness when he came to
me he had not gotten back more than
twenty-five per cent. of his former business.

When I showed him how he had used the
same law of unconscious imaging (but
with pictures and ideas directly opposite
to what he really wanted,) to destroy his

practice that he originally used to build it he at once realized this and went to work to rebuild under the Law of Harmonious Attraction, and within the next forty-five days it increased to four-fifths of as much as it ever had been.

Under this law the money we accumulate comes to us on a plane of consciousness so high that we cannot lose it, because no force is strong enough to displace the power we have under the Law of Harmonious Attraction.

Under this law we have power without force, while under the Law of Force we have force without power, other than such as might or force gives us. But under that Law there is always some stronger force, some stronger might, which rises up at most inopportune times and displaces our force, our might.

CHAPTER XIV.

" Vacant Space " Around Us is not Vacant.—
Man is Like a Central Telephone Station.
—What Connection do We Wish to Make?
—" Am I to Buy Something I Want but for
Which I Cannot Pay?"—Greatest Secret
in Life.—Experience of a New York City
Minister.—Who is the Successful Man?

This vacant space everywhere around
us is vacant only to our physical senses.
It contains the material, in solution, for
everything we have ever had materialized
in objective form, or ever will have.

When we have obtained the vision of an
abundance of supply and our *oneness* with
it, and have formed the *fixed habit* of holding fast to it, we make of ourselves a
magnet through which we relate with the
harmonious and constructive currents and

attract from this formless energy the
atoms which make for abundance of supply
in our lives.

We are all like a central telephone station. All around us is the switchboard
with wires leading out to every part of the
city, to the saloons, opium joints, broth-
els, and other places of degradation—these
represent the destructive forces; other
wires lead to the homes, churches, schools,
and everything which symbolizes the constructive power. Each one of these
wires has a socket while the operator has
a plug which when inserted in any one of
the sockets makes the connection complete. We can put the plug in a socket
which will connect us with the poverty-
stricken districts, the saloons, the opium
joints, etc., or we can put the plug in a
socket which will connect us with the

homes, the churches, the institutions of learning and higher places of culture.

WHAT CONNECTION DO WE WISH TO MAKE? One with the constructive powers or one with the destructive forces? The operator—our will-power—will connect us with either.

When the plug is jammed away in the connection is strong and complete, but when it only touches the socket the connection is slight and weak.

So with each life. We have invisible rays—wires—running out in all directions from us which touch all the currents of the universe. We stand in the center with our intellect ready to execute the command of our will-power. Our will-power—the central operator—acts in accordance with the images or thoughts—subscribers' calls— which we allow to persist. When we

live in or image—imagine—destructive
thoughts we relate with the currents in
which are located all the destructive
things, the same as when we connect
with any 'phone representing the destructive forces. It depends entirely upon
where we put the plug of our thoughts as
to what connection we make with these
numerous currents, and that determines
the relationship we establish.

When we put the plug in the thought
current of lack and poverty, when we say
or think or imagine, " I am poor," " I must
economize," " I cannot afford to do it," " I
am a lunkhead," or belittle ourselves in
any way, we recognize in our consciousness, by such thought or action, our separation from the abundance of supply, and
are creating a consciousness of poverty;
we are holding up a vision or image of lack

and through that very connection we attract from out this formless energy the
material which goes to make for lack and
poverty in our lives.

On the other hand when we put this
thought plug into the socket which con-
nects with the abundance of supply, when
we recognize that it is impossible for us to
have lack in our lives no matter how
poverty-stricken our objective environment
may be, when we *fill* our imagination with
the image of our oneness with the abundance of supply and hold this image continuously and persistently, we are creating a consciousness of *wealth and success,*
and we attract to us, by that very connection, the atoms from the formless energy
which begin to materialize this abundance
of supply in our environment.

One may ask, " Am I to go and buy something which I may want but for which I am not able to pay?" The proper attitude in such a case is this: Buy it in your thought world, *see* yourself owning it—that is imagine (image) your ownership of it—do this persistently and continuously in your thought world and in that way create a consciousness that it is yours NOW, recognize your *oneness* with it NOW and in accordance with your degree of *recognizing that oneness* will it materialize for you.

The greatest secret of life is RECOGNITION. From the moment we are born and instinctively turn to our mother's breast, recognizing that the life and sustenance for our physical body is to be found there, down to the period we call "death," we only get the things for our bodies and environment that we consciously or unconsciously recognize.

On the objective plane, when our income is limited, it is necessary to adjust our expenses to such limits as long as we retain the consciousness of limitation but there is no reason why we should retain that limitation in our consciousness. On the other hand there is every reason why we should at once go to work and develop a consciousnss which does not in any way recognize any limitations. That is one step towards removing the objective limitations.

When we have established the *fixed habit* in our lives of recognizing our oneness with everything we want, established it so firmly that it is just as *natural* as is the habit of breathing, then we will find that the way will be opened up on the objective plane for us to materialize whatever we may want just as rapidly as we determine that we really do want it and are willing to pay the price for obtaining it. The *price* to be paid under such conditions is to attract it to us under the Law of Harmony.

At a recent service in one of the New York churches the minister talked on "Faith." In order to illustrate his point he related the following incident. He was fond of playing golf; a small lake was one of the hazards on the links he used; he had made it many times and had never failed in the attempt. At the time of this incident and just as he was about to make the drive a friend said "Doctor, can you see the ball on the other side? Should you not be able to see it there it will fall in the lake." He made the drive and the ball fell into the lake. Why? Simply because he unconsciously allowed his friend's image of "seeing the ball fall into the lake" to displace his own image of " seeing the ball fall safely on the other shore." Had the friend given him the same image as his own, instead of giving him one of doubt, fear, anxiety or failure, the ball would have landed safely on the other shore as it always had done before.

Many times we have an image of success when some kind (?) friend, like that of the Doctor's, gives to us an image of doubt or failure and we unconsciously recognize it, instead of our own image of success, and failure is the inevitable result.

The man who is successful is the one who has *filled* his imagination with images, visions, and ideas of success, and who displaces as often as is necessary all thoughts and images of failure and lack which may come to him from every source.

There is never a moment of our lives but

what we are imagining or imaging something, and when we image lack in our
environment and our separation from the
abundance of supply, that is what we will
materialize; but when we learn to image
consciously and persistently the thing we
want, to *fill* our imagination with the abundance of supply, with the abundance of
money, of food, of clothing, of joy, of happiness, of success, and our *oneness* with it, it
is just as sure to materialize for us in form
on the objective plane, in accordance with
the degree and persistency with which we
intelligently apply these laws, as it is for
us to absorb the air into our lungs whenever we breathe.

CHAPTER XV.

SUMMARY OF THE UNIVERSAL LAWS WHICH MAKE
FOR SUCCESS.—WHY WE REFUSE TO ATTACK
ANY ONE.—THIS ATTITUDE DOES NOT TAKE
AWAY OUR INITIATIVE.—PERSONAL EXPERI-
ENCE OF THE AUTHOR.—WHY ALL PERSONS
LIVING WILL NOT BE SUCCESSFUL AT THE SAME
TIME.—WHO WILL BE SUCCESSFUL.—WILL
YOU BE ONE OF THEM?

The universal laws which make for success are the Law of Harmonious Attraction, the Law of Non-Resistance in its
positive application, the Law of Conscious
Imaging or Ideation, and the Law of Persistent Application.

Under the Law of Harmonious Attraction we take an attitude which will make
for harmony in our lives toward everything that comes to us. No matter how inharmonious has been our attitude in the

past we now refuse to let any person or any thing disturb our harmony. The moment we recognize that we are becoming inharmonious we at once change our attitude and get back under the Law of Harmony.

Under the positive application of the Law of Non-Resistance we stand firm, but not resistant nor resentful, for the application of the principles and laws which are constructive and harmonious in our lives and we defend our position and our attitude against the fiercest onslaughts which the destructive forces of the universe may make upon us, through people and things, but in our defence we are exceedingly careful that we do not step over the boundary line which divides defence from offence. We refuse to attack anyone or any thing, because the moment we attack we cease to defend and begin to offend, thus getting into the destructive currents and becoming destructive in our creations and materializations. This at-titude does not take away from us any of our initiative, but it does require that when we do take the initiative that our consciousness is free from all desire for re-venge, free from all resentment, resistance, etc.; that our only desire is to uphold what we believe to be constructive and harmo-nious and not to convert the " other fel-low " to our way of thinking. That the " other fellow " may take a destructive at-titude towards us is not our concern; it is his business not to do so and when he is not *big* enough to be constructive and harmo-nious in his attitude that is his misfortune and he will have to take what goes with it until he learns his lesson of harmony.

Under the Law of Conscious Imaging or Ideation, through our inspirational, intuitional, and revelational faculties, we create the vision or image of the thing we want and by the intelligent use of our intellect we hold fast to this vision or image in our thought world and begin its creation in material form by doing the things which we find nearest at hand to do on the objective plane, doing them with all our might, doing them harmoniously, constructively, and without resentment or resistance, knowing that each thing we do under these laws brings us one step nearer to the materialization of our vision.

Under the Law of Persistent Application we go on day after day holding fast to our image of success, not resenting nor resisting any apparent failure of its immediate materialization, working harmoniously and constructively under these laws without looking for results. When we look for results we relate with the currents in which doubt, fear, worry, anxiety, lack, etc., are found and such relationship delays the materialization of results.

When we have built a consciousness which will enable us to live under these laws without looking for results, but because they are so deeply stamped upon our own consciousness and have become such a *fixed habit* in our lives that they are a part of our character and are *natural* to us, when we live under these laws because they are the highest and greatest and best thing we know how to live and because we cannot live under any others, then will we become the master of ourselves and our environment, and success will be ours along every line we may direct.

Let me tell you of a personal experience which I had a number of years ago in my business in the commercial world and which illustrates the unconscious use I made of these laws. At that time I was doing business largely on borrowed capital and the time came when it was necessary for me to raise $1,000 by a certain date or lose $10,000. I had reached the limit of my borrowing capacity at my bank and so went to friends in my efforts to raise the money. Every avenue on the objective plane seemed to be closed against me and nowhere did I receive any encouragement in the way of assistance.

I had made up my mind in the beginning, however, that I would raise the $1,000 and would not lose my $10,000 and no matter how often I met with a refusal I persisted in affirming that I had the money NOW.

As the days went by, and every avenue on the objective plane seemed closed to me, I made my affirmation that much stronger and more powerful, were it possible to do so, displacing instantly every thought of fear, anxiety, doubt, etc., refusing to allow them to find lodgment in my thought world.

The morning of the day upon which I had to pay the $1,000 arrived and without my having either the money or any idea from where it would come. As I walked down to my office that morning I said: "It has come to a showdown, for this is the day I must make the payment. I do not know from where the money is coming, but I do know that some way will be opened up to me and that is all I need know."

When I opened my mail I found a letter from one of my friends, to whom I had previously applied for the loan but who had not been able to let me have it at that time, enclosing his check for $1,000 and so I was saved.

This is what had occurred: A man who had owed him several thousand dollars paid the indebtedness before it was due and my friend, knowing my need, at once sent me the $1,000.

" Pure luck and just a matter of chance " the unthinking world would say, but it was nothing of the kind. I had the inspiration that somewhere I would get that money. My intuition told me to hold fast to that belief and so I used my intellect to hold my conscious mind—the image in my imagination—in accordance with that inspiration and belief and to shut out from my thought world anything which would in any way impair that image.

The result was that the Universal Law, manipulating as it does people and things to accord with our vision—our image—caused this third party, who was entirely unknown to me, to pay his indebtedness before it was due and then have my friend send the amount I wished to borrow.

Had I allowed my intellect to dim the vision, the image, which my inspirational, intuitional, and revelational faculties gave me, had I allowed that vision, that image, to waver and permitted one instead which said it was impossible for me to get the money, I never would have gotten it, never could have gotten it, because the Universal Law manipulates people and things in accordance with the energy we generate in our thought world through the use we make by our intellect of our inspirational, intuitional and revelational faculties.

Were it possible to impart to the consciousness of all mankind this great truth, were it possible to stamp it upon the intelligence of each atom in the body and environment of every life, then teach each one how to apply it and develop in them the power or understanding of its application, poverty, lack, sorrow, misery, one and all, would be immediately banished from the face of the earth forever.

But this is not possible at the present time because we are all in such different states of unfoldment and we could just as well expect to teach every child how to solve problems in geometry and higher mathematics the moment it enters the kindergarten as we could expect to teach every life these greater truths and their power of application at once in their present state of unfoldment.

Some lives will immediately begin to absorb, digest, assimilate and make them their own, not because they are smarter or possess any greater power than do the lives which do not understand and therefore cannot at the present time assimilate these truths, but simply because the first class of lives have already developed these several faculties to a greater extent and the relationship between them is more harmonious in such lives.

The children in consciousness—those who have not yet developed these faculties —not only can do so but will do so somewhere down the line of their cosmic journey, and the sooner they begin to live in and practice these truths the sooner will such lives become the masters of themselves and their environment.

No matter how old we may be in years

in this incarnation, no matter how wasted and spent and useless our lives seem to have been, it is never too late to begin. No matter how weak and puny and puerile our lives and our efforts may seem to us to have been, just know this, *know it beyond any question of a doubt, that we one and all possess within us all the great wonderful creative power of the universe and it is simply a matter of getting that power out into harmonious expression to enable us to become masters of ourselves and our environment under the Law of Harmonious Attraction, and attract success to us along any line we may wish. WILL YOU BE ONE TO DO IT NOW?*

www.ingramcontent.com/pod-product-compliance
Lightning Source LLC
Chambersburg PA
CBHW080505110426

42742CB00017B/2998